PARALLEL PLAY

Other Books by Stephen Burt

POETRY

Popular Music

CRITICISM

Randall Jarrell and His Age

Randall Jarrell on W. H. Auden (co-edited with Hannah Brooks-Motl)

Parallel Play

POEMS

Stephen Burt

Graywolf Press
SAINT PAUL, MINNESOTA

Publication of this volume is made possible in part by a grant provided by the Minnesota State Arts Board, through an appropriation by the Minnesota State Legislature; a grant from the Wells Fargo Foundation Minnesota; and a grant from the National Endowment for the Arts, which believes that a great nation deserves great art. Significant support has also been provided by the Bush Foundation; Target, with support from the Target Foundation; the McKnight Foundation; and other generous contributions from foundations, corporations, and individuals. To these organizations and individuals we offer our heartfelt thanks.

MINNESOTA
STATE ARTS BOARD

NATIONAL
ENDOWMENT
FOR THE ARTS

Supported by the Jerome Foundation in celebration of the Jerome Hill Centennial and in recognition of the valuable cultural contributions of artists to society

Published by Graywolf Press
2402 University Avenue, Suite 203
Saint Paul, Minnesota 55114
All rights reserved.

www.graywolfpress.org

Published in the United States of America

ISBN 1-55597-437-6

2 4 6 8 9 7 5 3 1
First Graywolf Printing, 2006

Library of Congress Control Number: 2005932353

Cover design: Kyle G. Hunter

Cover photograph: Berenice Abbott, Murray Hill Hotel from Park Avenue and 40th Street, Manhattan. November 19, 1935. © Photography Collection, Miriam and Ira D. Wallach Division of Art, Prints and Photographs, The New York Public Library, Astor, and Tilden Foundations

To the memory of Samuel Burt,
and of Esther Burt Heller,
and of Millard Cass.
And to Ruth Marx Cass.

CONTENTS

I

II

III

IV

ACKNOWLEDGMENTS

Many of these poems have appeared (sometimes in earlier versions, or with different titles) in or via these journals and programs, in print or on the web: *AGNI*, *American Letters & Commentary*, *Avatar Review*, *Barrow Street*, the *Bloomsbury Review*, the *Blue Moon Review*, *Boston Review*, *CHAIN*, *Colorado Review*, *dislocate*, *Elixir*, *Explosive*, *Free Verse*, *Fuori*, *Gulf Coast*, the *Hartford Courant*, *Jacket*, *LUNA*, *Maisonneuve*, *McSweeney's Online*, *newmediapoets.com*, the *Paris Review*, *Ploughshares*, *PN Review*, the *Portland Review*, *www.poems.com*, *Poetry Matters*, *Poetry Review*, *Post Road*, *Slope*, *Tabla*, *thepage.name*, *Thumbscrew*, *Times Literary Supplement*, *Web del Sol*, *Word of Mouth* (Minnesota Public Radio), and the *Yale Review*. Four poems appeared in the chaplet *Brief History of American Youth* (Minneapolis: WinteRed, 2004). "The New Rock Jen" appeared in *Wild and Whirling Words* (Silver Spring, MD: Etruscan, 2004). "Paysage Moralisé" and "Morningside Park" appeared in *Legitimate Dangers: American Poets of the New Century* (Lexington, KY: Sarabande, 2006). My thanks to all these entities, and to their editors.

For practical and institutional support, I am grateful to Stuart McDougal and Macalester College; to Rachel Hadas, the Loft, and the McKnight Foundation; and to Team Graywolf, especially Jeff, Fiona, Mary, and J.

Too many trusted friends read and reacted to these poems, and to the work that preceded them, for me to list them all. I am, however, particularly grateful to Jordan Ellenberg, Forrest Gander, Nick Halpern, Saskia Hamilton, Ange Mlinko, John Redmond, Amanda Schaffer, Michael Scharf, C. D. Wright, Jane Yeh, and Monica Youn.

And—as always, and forever—to Jessica Bennett.

I

She turned back to the ghosts, who were thronging closer and closer.

"Please!" they were whispering. "You've just come from the world! Tell us, tell us! Tell us about the world!"

—Philip Pullman, *The Amber Spyglass*

BLUEBELLS

Purple, in fact, they sprint up the length of our street
and back down through a pair of bicycle tires,
then run themselves to ground amid the heat
of broken flag and flagstone and cement.
Sun turns them down. Air shakes them in their tiers,
correcting their posture, composing their migrant scent.

The bright albino squirrels
we saw again this morning make a sort
of couple, like Hepburn and Grant. Their last resort,
as they scramble around one another and around
their own mercurial tails,
becomes a cleft between two trunks, so dark
nobody could inspect it from the ground:

it could hold rubies, coded maps, a child.
Now that we've spent
a year on Fairmount Avenue, such heady sights remind
me less of balmy days in Central Park
and more of a rock star from Iceland, who lived in a tent
for a year in a climate-controlled New York apartment
in order to think of the wind, the cold, the wild.

LIKE A WRECK

Flaunting your useless knowledge has failed you again,
Though it was all they had taught you. Worse yet,
Those self-demotions had always worked
In emergencies before; now they seemed about
To succumb to a Coriolis-cum-Peter
Principle: each fact sinks
Until you have to dredge it up and get
Away with it before it can start to trouble
The ruffled surface of the dream you share.

So once again, they've run you out of
Town on a toy train. It all seems pleasant:
These clapboard shrubs and candybox pastels
Part where the heathers wave back at us. Do they know?
A folded hillside saves snow; it shines like diapers,
Parts and shows
The larch you noticed the last time you wet your pants.
It was a Thursday. The tall teacher cleared the room
As sunlight shocked the prurient glass doors . . .

The tracks ahead continue to choke and spurt.
When were you alive? New shoes won't help.
Neither will asking the right questions. Maybe a ring . . .
To stay in your present tense, and keep your promise,
We'll have to clear these girders off you first.

RACHEL NEWCASTLE: *DIPTYCH: GIRL AND DIARY*

Between the ocean and the flat garage
September gives itself away; its streaks
Of rusty sun sweep up the day beside
The boy who curls in patchy sleep behind
The squat vacation bungalows. Up front,
      This girl who's slept away the afternoon
Could fall for someone like him, but not him,
Or not just now. She shivers, stands
And stretches out; her sweatshirt sheds its sand.
She balances her journal in one hand:

The trouble is, when you're not anything
You think you could be all kinds of things
And then you choose. And then you are one thing
And nothing else is you—the other things
You could have been aren't yours to keep or say.
      Wind tweaks her collar, rattles her long sleeves;
This summer is a drag. Waves disappoint
Her as she turns to walk indoors
Into the second panel, where she stoops
And tries to feel at home. Behind her back

The stairs crowd up like answers, and the row
Of things she owns or made has the hard face
And subsea glitter of a coral reef;
Unset alarm clock, pastel candles, brash
And sticker-plastered daybook, types and wards
      Or warders of a life
Where nothing has gone permanently wrong,
Extend as if for good below the long
Bay window she turns toward,
The sunstruck frame in which she sees herself

Half-lost in the large world of settled things:
The plum-branch clawing at a leaf-
Clogged roof, the weeds along the crew-cut yard,
The phone poles' slanting stilts, and, farther off,
The water towers like the aliens
       In books her older brother used to read,
Who walked the earth in huge metallic tripods,
Snapped high-strung bridges, broke apart the roads
And kicked in half the roofs of baseball domes
Before succumbing to the common cold.

OUR SUMMER JOBS

A lemon or a candy-lemon slice,
The moon comes out to tantalize the boys.

Our elders insisted nutrition comprise our appeal.
Yet once, behind the pet store, after school...

Then you wore shoes, and the moment was lost for good.
Our hopes now lay in nightly rendezvous

Behind the confectionery stand, or in the accountants'
Crawlspace. There, above the projection booths,

We could pretend to be conducting business,
Counting out talents, validating our prey.

It hasn't been our work to decide what's important.
We are offended because we haven't been asked,

Although we don't want them. Split in the hurry-up dawn,
We suck on our Merits, awaiting our buses; the novel

Morning scowls back at us, awed by our brazen disdain.

SELF-PORTRAIT AS KITTY PRYDE

I have been identified
as gifted & dangerous. People fight over me
but not in the ways I want. Who would expect
it in a girl from Deerfield, Illinois,
town of strict zoning, no neon & quality schools?
I pass through difficult physical laws, cement,
flames, cupboards, crowds, tree trunks & arguments,
precociously, like something to protect.
I am always going through some phase.

My best friend spent apprentice years
alone inside a study like a star.
My wide eyes & Jewish hair
are shyness, a challenge to artists, &
untouchable. I can slip out of the back of a car.
When I am tired I dance, or pace
barefoot on the civilian ground
of Salem Center, where rain falls through me.
I have begun to learn to walk on air.

Adventures overemphasize my age.
In my distant & plausible future I will bear
one child, scorn, twenty-five pounds
of technology on my back, & the further weight
of giving orders to a restless band
of misfits who save America from its own rage
but cannot save themselves, & stay up late.
My friends & the fate of the world will have come to rest,
unexpected, staccato, in my sophomore hands.

MOSCOW FOR TEENS

Our borrowed kitten, black and white like ice,
Chases full bottles of aspirin and makes no sound.

Summer is hard to see through: slags of dust
Deform the coppery air. Orioles in the elms . . .

St. Michael roams the curbs and perezhods,
Handing out his weapons of bruised fruit;

Here pushcarts vend fresh water, sausages,
Blackcurrants, figs my uncle refuses to touch.

Below the university, every evening,
The etiolated business districts shine:

A scowling boy splays over the high railing
Where no one wants to watch. Late that same night

We see the lit domes in the brief dark, but read instead
About the great comedian Behemoth,

The black cat from *The Master and Margarita*,
Whose toothy swagger cuts the concrete sky.

CANAL PARK DRIVE

"ultra-oligotrophic"

Here we are in Duluth. They have remade
The strenuous, swept edges of the largest
Body of fresh water in the world
So we would come and visit, and we
Did: above our heads
Some bradycardic boxcars pull
Their taconite over their trestles, then over
And underneath the shadow of the bluff . . .

To ask the kids *(So do you hate it here?)*
Or question the slow clouds *(Where would you go?)*
Would show the same broad hopes, and would betray
Us *(Where could all the girders lead?)*
As if we meant to offer something else.

Refreshment, strong air, onions frying, hops.
A brand-new stage recumbent on a pier
Where brand-new wheelchair ramps describe floodwalls.
Fresh waters plane the middle distances
Like seminal regrets,
Are interrupted by one buoy, one boat;
Gulls shift, declaim and moralize, and these
First lineaments of rain
Simply continue, as if testing old
Adages on the origin of us,
Propelled as we are by whispers, and whispered hints
That here is some place we would rather be.

PAYSAGE MORALISÉ

Mom and Dad must have believed they had found a safe place:
The ten- and twelve-year-olds they could place
In the neighborhood schools, the teens who would take their place
In a few years, and the young adults who would replace
Themselves if all went well could each find a place
In this frivolous landscape, which nonetheless offered no place
Without its form of scrutiny. Sneakers displaced
The gravel and kicked open a secret place
Under the storm drain, its covers yanked back into place
Above the echoing concrete; a tourney took place
Around the one basketball hoop. It was no place
To write home about, but it wasn't your place
To complain: you nearly lost your place
In the slow novel of your own life (date and place
Of publication unknown) in which you place
As a supporting character. Mark your place
With a match, shut the book, and attend: "I've been running in place,"
Said Ellen, meaning just that her displays
Of mental acuity seemed to have taken place
Not as stunts, nor as ends in themselves, only as place-
Holders for later goals she could never quite place
In her own field of view, but sped towards, hoping to place
In the annals of distance running, as if to plac-
Ate the team on which the whole town plays.
You, on the other hand, have kept your place
In the bleachers complac-
Ently . . . Look: they sprint towards Kate's new place,
As sunlight keeps them, in its sewn-up lace,
Content with a kiss, a trophy for second place,
And everything you would want, had you once stood in their place.

PIERRE BONNARD: *STANDING NUDE*

Glossy lime, amethyst, rosewater, mother-of-
Pearl: what other than color stays alive
And under the sun to love? The tall flat
Mirror I see for myself has been left out
Of the picture you approach, and the giggly, mild
Children who gather together in my
Field of view, then chase each other away,
Their vinyl coats scraping and swishing, can never hold
My interest as I might keep theirs; my gold-
Flecked sides have gone bare for so many summers that I
Can shrug off their gazes with ease as I do
My hair. Once I rang in the brave new
Year as the belle of a country ball, who now
Face all day the severity of a Mission-
Style rocking chair; I look askance
At a minor Degas (very minor) as she strains
To pull on her new tights. Her poiseless
Poise, forever off balance
Through no fault of her own, shows how her lot
Is cast: she means to fit
Them perfectly, or die in the attempt.
The copper-blue-nailed, violet-haired, contempt-
Uous guard who covers her rippling yawn
Comes closer than any admirer to my own
Sang-froid: each day I watch an ever-gaudier
Sun (itself unseen) embroider
The robes I will never pick up, in band over band
Of opalescent sparks. I stand behind
A door I will never pass through, and all I have
To keep to myself are times when visitors leave,
And colors I know, by now, like the back of my hand.

FOR LINDSAY WHALEN

You only have the skills that you can use.
The shots you make surround you like a breeze.
When someone wins, then someone has to lose.

You don't show off. We know you by your moves:
A feint, a viewless pass, a perfect tease
Make space for all the skills that you can use.

Defenders and their shadows, three on two,
Start at you like infuriated bees:
You glide through them. You take the looks they lose.

As serious as science, picking clues
And dodges that no other player sees,
You find the skills that only you could use:

Applause, then silence. Scrape of distant shoes.
Then race through packed periphery to free
Space no one lifts a hand to. —Win or lose,

Such small decisions, run together, fuse
In concentration nothing like the ease
We seem to see in all the skills you use,
Till someone wins. Then someone else will lose.

HELP WITH YOUR PLANT QUESTIONS

You could take it from here, on these curt rocks' cut-glass court
Before the allspice tree whose anxious bark
Peels and grows back in wires; from its height
We may remain visible only as strict
Connoisseurs, defenders of no ground.
Politics lends us our interest, but it won't last,
Nor outlast these older possessors, who knew
Where to look: your learning curve, Janel, is one

These cycads bear into their microclimates, grids
Of desperate fronds and all that they survey
Who make the nets in which to catch the hopes
Whose souvenirs they bring us. Are you
Certain of your own heart? Are
You certain who cares? Who bred you, and should
You take up the purpose for which they gladly served
Or press down, like roots, for a confident repeal

Of all your fibrous parents took away
From spoiled loam in their old country? The ripe
And vigorous bottle and solitaire, giants among
Palms, arrive with their varied and expert advice
About growing up taller next time: consider this
Life as a sport, the prize hidden, the rules introduced
Too late for us to learn them all, the score
Untied at the half, the quickness that gives

Advantage loose, rolling away far under the sun,
Though only within these green boundaries do we still
Live and remain uncertain of love, point
Taken. For the brain is a
Bromeliad, and that fig tree, hacked away
So that it grows back orderly next season,
Has become your good harbinger: nothing is safe,
Nothing accomplished, none yours, till the last sound blooms.

SCENES FROM NEXT WEEK'S *BUFFY THE VAMPIRE SLAYER*

The rolls of carpet come out in all colors:
Apparently unsalable, they lean
Against the Sunnydale Tool
And Magic Shop—then up
In smoke they go: show the whole block on fire,
Then cut to Faith, who's smiling. She's to blame.
And here come the credits. Later the star of the show

Could arrive, see vamps, warn all, stand out,
Snap a fence post in half, and start
To fence with it. O foleys, do your work:
We want to be half-fooled. That good can win
And isn't always ugly, that sleek fish
Were athletes once, werewolves play Fender Strats
And souls are round like geodes inside-out

Has to be true for these dusty particulars
To be like somewhere we would choose to live:
Otherwise the closed shop is, simply, closed
For good and business reasons, morning made
Of risible schedules, babysitting and cash,
The script not censored or altered after all
But the work of a number 2 pencil moving along

With several thousand others in their wooden
Tiers on Saturday, blackening
Old questions that arrange us for our roles
In plots on TV shows, on the narrow channels
Nobody would choose, if she thought she could have a choice.

BRIEF HISTORY OF NORTH AMERICAN YOUTH

Spring pinches as it enters in the style of a foreign

eye or garment quizzically over the market's final square

outdoors the household keeps warm keeping in

the ancient of days the last novices practice their weave

their crabapples and their demography barricades

against the inexplicable the roar

of the material victory whose bracing

final snow abandons every year

❂

Short hair did not require the same kind of labor

and visually separated the young as would

defenses greater height long boots and bangs

and so the grid over the map of America knots

where loose strands tied not wanting to become

the first generation to take only what they could

or what they were promised an echo an aunt decades back

why must we turn a profit lest we die

❂

I will sew and read all the time I am not going out

anywhere but intend to stay home all the time

Resolved not to talk about myself or my feelings . . .

Repentance is good but it should not distract one's thoughts

I have got into a very bad habit of trying

to sift myself out and find out what there is of me

On my birthday I am going to try

to turn over a new leaf and be a new girl

❁

Our students enchant themselves now to stop traffic their rhyme

reverberates over the rush hour blanching thin leaves

like bells and drums collective certainties

I want to take you back Dan Treacy sang

not laughing *to the Sixties and leave you there*

Congratulations Kate your ribbon must

have come from the march this morning *No it's for*

my friend Callie she died a year ago today

❁

Who learned the rope trick who learned to get back on defense

who learned to race through the transition to handle some world

as if it were one ball to take two steps

before it leaves the hand spectators crush

and shout together standing up exclaim

taut echo chamber painted wordless space

for relays or derision or a fall

we will know who we are once we have won

❁

Who waited who would have been wanted who waits there still

his green beat-up car until the sun came up

who noticed both of you and let

you in the sycamore leaves

of Bethesda cover their grounds

for pale majestic sophomore jealousy

on their discarded branches swans and tests

and outgrown exclamations warm at dawn

❁

Still there a constellation every year

the hands at Hains Point reach up in half dark

like technical giants we buried still misunderstood

amid them rites of spring their volume raised

asking *what did they give up to get here and how long ago*

do you miss it at all does it suit you did it then

what does it say in what language for how long

will you talk back to it can it hear what does it sing

AFTER CALLIMACHUS

Cover me quietly, stone.
I wrote verse. I meant little in life,
blamed few and injured none;
I tried to get along.
My writings kept me warm.
If I with my featherlight pen
confused prestige with worth,
praised evil, or ever wronged
the few who wanted a fight,
allow me, generous earth,
to do no further harm—
let me atone in my sleep;
I with my good will,
so lightly and often given,
who rest with nothing to keep,
and nothing to offer heaven.

II

I thought, as I have many times in the concourse, that if I were a stranger to this overwhelming city, it would be helpful to me to know that something in me and in everyone around me already knew how to fit in with all the people circulating through the city and going about their business. After emerging onto Vanderbilt Avenue, I found that when I crossed over and walked along the south side of Forty-third Street, I could for a while keep with me this awareness of the cooperation that makes a city possible. It lasted about a block and a half . . .

—Tony Hiss, *The Experience of Place*

CATHEDRAL PARKWAY SUBWAY GRATE

Like stars   *   like stars
among the shackles and the grid
none of us fit   *   spectacular stars
in the midst of oversized snow
a heaven of differences
blown through the grate both ways   *   on New Year's Day
the lives we have   *   have had
circulating   *   blown
fastidious up and back again   *   in the midst
of glint   *   of street above   *   of schedules
of the artifice of   *   the old year   *   of one night's
accomplishment   *   a train   *   a train   *   a train

POSTCARD SENT ON NEW YEAR'S DAY

The Ancients remain in our building.
                                    Ash in their air;
a quota of dead pigeons in our path.

The rewards come slow,
                    the difficulties like a spate of glass:
all over the sidewalk, and still on the scene.
We too will be punished, but not yet.

The variegated bricks set up next door,
the little aerie hewn above the stairs,

are a twelve-tone scale: slight
                                things, small charms,
the jagged ones you have to learn to hear.

A LONG WALK ON A WEEKDAY AFTERNOON

The NEW YORK CITY FIRE MUSEUM names
the men who died on ladders, and the men
who invented the modern system of volunteers.
Throughout the 1700s, porcelain
"fire marks," attached to certain structures,
meant blazes extinguished there would bring a reward.

❋

Such public space: sun bangs on every sill
at Spring and Van Dam, at Charles and Greenwich streets.
Privately, you'd live there if you could.

❋

Defunct refrigerators form a row
on the sunlit walks, their backs peeled
up and off like rusted tins of fish.

And televisions in a spell of rain
lie face down on one stoop, their backs sheared off
so that each picture tube points up towards air,
its wires stuck out: disabled, or exposed.

❋

The tiger-striped awning at GIRLPROPS.COM,
formerly known as SO WHAT?,
shades rhinestone rings like icing on pink cake:
"funner," a customer says
agreeably, "than the real thing," as they are.

❋

Then comes the call you've waited for all day:
there's nothing in
him any more, or nothing
worth the cost of the pursuit.

Two silk ties, cement-grey or dove-grey,
cling to an otherwise-empty aluminum rack,
behind thick glass: curved, sunlit, shatterproof.

July 2001

TENTH AVENUE

The peregrine iron
Creeper buoys
Its bricks; their scaffolds face up to the air.
The hush files in from the Hudson, the roar from points east.
Flip the lids up on your sunglasses: "It's a new world."

Its rooftop holds:
The horizontal glare, the overheard joke,
The scraps of a bill in the wind, the far-fetched birds,
The action you can't call selfish, the van that sputs
And pulls away, speckled and matte like a tangerine rind.

A sadness of missed, of just-missed expectations
Startles the Meat District's rainy biers:
This is the world to come. All your decisions
Are yours now, to be made over again.
No one will tell you when you get them right.

STEAM

Something substantial

and uncontrolled, false

starts, a lover's down-

town coming into view—

like a game of charades
played with, or by, the sun—

the taller boy
with freckles is your past—

the ovals on the paving stones, your

technical and profitable future—

You make a phone call

or no phone call, this ordinary

day like one dictated in a dream—

its outdoor

faces and thighs, municipal

fountains, belt buckles, and fallen, half-winged
gingko leaves and leavings, stay

and cannot give you leave

      to go inside, and are

all that they seem—

MORNINGSIDE PARK

Without fear or fault, the green
Expanse of it drops off at acute
Angles, sudden and inconveniently,
Till laden branches bless the rest of the boulevard.
Here you too may mail a letter abroad
Or unfold laundry,
Perform essential services, clip shade
In transient humidity.
                              Bedazzled,
Like a friend you've missed for years, except
That he doesn't know who you are, nor want to,
This puffy guy jogs up
Then down, then up the stairs.
I want to cry
At all costs: look, quick wind, I'm one of you!
But each afternoon
The sun strikes, as in bowling,
And all is cleared away, although the wind
Competes: it cleans its area, then punches
Out as night comes on
And drops off the residues, rainily, later, in Queens,
Among the distant congregations. Somebody
Trots a cat on a leash; the smaller
Mutts look up a bit, unnerved,
And prance up, almost bounce, on their back legs,
Having their very
Own vertiginous day.

Nothing I do can satisfy those I care for.
Appropriate flowers grow harder and harder to find.

BERENICE ABBOTT'S NEW YORK

Is it a vanishing point or is it
      Brooklyn into which the cables run

      Brooklyn over which these two
      these shadowy walkers come

      against the shaded rails against

      the future in the arcades in the bridge

      the parallels above them in midair

Under a clatter of fire-escapes
                          slick mist
      a wooden sign   MAC-LAC SHELLAC

      At Cliff and Ferry streets
      the Bank of New York spire flanks its skies

      One horse-drawn cart already obsolescent

      perseveres on its last cobbled round

So much washing! whites and socks and shorts
      and jerseys, hand-towels, collars; X- and J-
      shaped cords cat's-cradle over raked-up ground
      between the model tenements   Such ragged work
      laid open in midair   and never done

The fashion forward Murray Hill Hotel's
    Art Nouveau nearly-spiral

                balcony
    connects and seems
          to spin
                a vaudeville turn
    Here all things have their promise
              steel and time
    So turn the globe
        to midtown now
             Look out
    Invite us up
        Let every daughter in

Some Studebakers and the mild
    sun cross over the Triborough Bridge together

    Someone should have warned us   Automobiles
    spare tires on their backs
    armed scouts   arrive equipped

    to spy out the land of Canaan
    the people that dwell therein

    and what land and what cities they might be

THE NEW ROCK JEN

at 9
pm tonight kicks out
slow burns, betrayals, anything the Chills
complained about, & buries them as evergreen
news stories might be
buried & she can get on

(O polychrome) & go out; new jewel tones,
recombinant noise, cool tomes, floor toms, some steep
raked stage's cornucopia of dates
& pomegranates, grasshoppers or
metropolitans, become her: now Interpol search
for her and not the reverse,

& there is that half-finished grid
still going up at Ninth and 43rd (O streaky sunset, O analog
eve) where something to see
has been seen through & will
be overcome. Avenue lights
entice all the more in the mist,

& though Godfrey adheres to the old
& admires a stranger just once in a decade, the new
rock Jen whose flair or
flare
of secrets nobody can hold
all by herself, moves once

(O sneakers, O velour
accessories) into her non-
stop plan *(each evening
the sun sets in 5 billion places)* under
ground, making the B
line work for her, out under the slangy sky.

AT THE BOWERY BALLROOM

Their spotlight jumps the nervy, packed-in fans
In the near-dark; its effervescent disc
Skips up the mezzanine, across barrettes'
Broad rhinestone squares as stones ride over streams.
                    The drum machine
Kicks out across the bars; the cool
Kids crowd up front or link hands. Crackle and glow—
            If it's a new beginning
                Then I don't
                Want to know—
Discretion and ambition and distraction
And all the daytime world a cancelled stamp—
            If it's not worth pretending
                Then I don't
                Want to know—
Your silver trainers with no laces hold
Whatever matters in the lower world
If only you would dance in them.
                            Who won't
Stand up for happy endings? Who would wait
To count the projectionist's spokes on the color wheel?
                Who couldn't spare
An hour, or a week, or a drab year?
                As on a dare,
The jet stream brings the air from Glasgow in;
                The next notes glide
Along the boards' auroras, down to where
                We stand—a kind
                Of glee: the beats
Close over us, reverse, cut back, begin.

AMARETTO SOUR (DRAG NIGHT AT THE NINES)

Your very own silver tights
Sag slightly after a kick
And Marta has her eye on Murray Hill.
Anonymous "space-age bachelor pad"
Extravagance, 3/4 time,
The velvet whirl of scarlet
Pleats (serve cold, with orange and cherry or lime)—

Above the New York Eye
And Ear Hospital, the dawn
Breaks promises, its coffee turns to cream,
The bubble machine
Steals summer from its balcony and sends
The rebels or revelers off
Their pedestals and home in awkward threes,
Through proclamations from the queen of queens;
Monday will see
The Cointreau and Grand Marnier
At rest on their high shelves,
The falsies back in their box, the mirror-ball rings
And feathery bangles away

And all of us our daylight selves. But now
And for a few sides yet,
In pink lipstick and pastel cigarettes
You are the girl for whom such things are done:
In jaunty stares, in rapid, amateur
And crowded dips and Spanish pirouettes
You spin because everything does. You will
Strike poses counterclockwise, re-
Invent the youth you grieve:
Last sliver of ice in a glass, last minute of play,
The ninth-grade girl who called, but never asked you out,
Or the boy who never gave you the time of day.

MOVING DAY

> . . . as if the battered old furniture that seemed so kindly, and the old carpets on which she had played, had been nourishing a secret grudge against her, and were not to be trusted any more.
>
> —Willa Cather, *The Song of the Lark*

Scraps and small reminders said the scissors to the shelf
Why do I feel empty said the oven to itself
Some of us are hungry said can opener to tin
Tell me said the radio *how much you want to win*
    And take us along when you go.

All the way from Thailand said the topmost row of cans
Rise and turn around again explained the standing fan
None of us are broken said the tumblers to the towel
Scratch me up or polish me said bannister to dowel
    And take us along when you go.

When they come to get you said a carton to its box
Count your lucky hours said a doorjamb to its locks
Will she will he will she sang the plumbing to the void
Did you mean to build me will I ever be destroyed

Carpet said to ceiling *Can I offer any more*
Nothing I can give you said the lintel to the door
You always overlook me said the baseboard to the stair
Board game valise said the attic *and a folding chair*
    And take us along when you go.

ON THE 'A'

Puzzled but admiring,
we watch the subway shaft ahead of us—
trestle and frame, frame, trestle and trestle and frame—
as if it were the approach
of the dreadful amphetamine night.
Then they call us back, and we are restored
to old expectancies: tomato-colored
luggage packed, another's hullabaloo
on a cell phone, as if announcing,
                    "What I have figured out
cannot wait for me to leave the shower
and dry myself with one of your terrycloth robes;
in fact, it is more important
that anything else in the world,
except for these postcards." How I have missed you all!
As we enter the air, one story over ground,
totemic heads pass, each like one sixteenth-note,
and scraps of chewed-up page, as if by the dog—
who didn't mean to do it, loveable thing,
and not quite used to the momentum.
Here in the realms of smoke, of ex-smokestacks,
we know we are already leaving; there remains
so little, like a bruise, that we can keep
that we are always deciding whether we want
to give it to local charity.
                    How alone
it is, therefore, to be with someone else,
whether facing the shore together, as over the rail
of a ferry in rain, or confusing
the banded, overlapping wooden planks
along one side of a tea-shop's battered sign
with the gnarled and tawny face of an indigent sailor

as the squat, brick blocks that herald the airport approach.
"In any case," the subway seems to say,
humming as it does while leaving New York
and crying at each stop, "We love you all
so much that we have difficulty parting
even from those we dislike,
from whom we might have learned, but never did,
these singularly wasted recent days;
nevertheless, we love you, we love you all."

AFTER CALLIMACHUS

Bunting I like, but not Olson, nor Bernstein, nor Pound;
  I'm tired of flashy long poems
that mean whatever anyone wants them to mean.
I'm also tired of crowds,
  hate the Met as I hate Times Square,
and won't see movies everyone else has seen.
As for you, Lusianias,
  I wanted to get to know you. Then I heard
how many others have known you, and how well.
Tomorrow, in fact, I suspect
  you'll show yet another young man
why he's just the one for you, and how you can tell.

III

Curiously, though, the times did not depress us. On the contrary, there was an exhilaration in Washington, a feeling that things were being mended, that great wrongs were being corrected, that there were no problems so big they wouldn't yield to the application of good sense and hard work. . . . There was a unifying source of inspiration, a great intelligence at work. It was called the New Deal and we were proud to be in on it.

—Roy Stryker, "The FSA Collection of Photographs"

SIXES AND SEVENS

> Durante la noche el Gobierno está en crisis total.
>
> —Ramón Gómez de la Serna, *Greguerías*

First snow this year a scratch across familiar grounds
       And the entire country up in the air.

For instance, the grimacing man in the Lake Street laundromat
       Who kicks and slaps the polished change machine

As if to force its slot to function, or to yield
       Him more than his one-dollar bill could give;

And faces on gray billboards, in gray contracting light
       With Fifties buildings cast like rows of dice

For traveling gamblers: *Better luck next time*.
       New ski boots print small drifts across the road;

Trunks open and shut, car opened and opened and shut
       In the blurred cold. November 8, heads down,

We carry all our baskets in our unprotected hands,
       Trying not to slip on the fresh ice.

THANKSGIVING 2002

The government froze, and then
we found it hard to breathe.
Bus stops where no one spoke
remembered other queues,
where flyers underfoot
dissolved like garlands, or
the ghosts of a belief—
of willful false belief.
Once we were on TV;
we counted, and we lost.
Apparently permanent clouds
blew in, and funereal bells,
and then the freezing rain.

This month the lots of rain
meant thumbs down and warped wood,
doorbells in Cottage Grove.
How often can you trust?
Twenty-nine percent
of those eligible, I
salute you. Sunset struck
late voters from their lots.

The people I came to like,

who slogged through wind all day,

and traffic, could almost drown

in one another's thin air.

Against the morning air,

I sat in our car and cried.

Heart, do not give your heart;

better to follow a sport,

where telling the truth won't hurt.

For how could you compete,

Being honor bred, with one

Who, were it proved he lies,

Were neither shamed in his own

Nor in his neighbor's eyes?

Only the fine art

of replacing the pins on a map

could save us, and even that

seemed almost entirely lost.

Obscured and almost lost

amid commercial hosts,

the Origins poster read

Win the Cold War. We tried

a water-painting kit,

whose strokes fade like applause.

The last drawbridge outdoors

stood lonely, and to scale

it seemed almost antique,

while taxicabs passed, and vans,

unwilling to give, backed up,

sounding their *basso* horns.

The fabled Gates of Horn . . .

On the way to their airport, the glow-

ing glow-in-the-dark signs point

straight up before the night.

Who owns the state? Who will?

Jets boom and stagger west.

Drivers, you hope for more

and self-sufficient lives.

When you are sick or alone

or miss the city, what

will you discover you want?

What will you tell the men

who own your roads by then?

i.m. Paul Wellstone (1944–2002)

THE ROAD BUILDERS

Nothing is spared.
The prayerful, seemingly rickety high
Radio towers let the wind beseech
Them; their popular waves
Pass through us & do not touch
The prominence of an otherwise-empty
Sky, where they arraign

Us not for the cities we had
But for those we could have.
These children picking up sticks
In their grandmother's roadside yard assemble them
Into a boundary, miniature
Protector: A-frame, imagined bedroom
Window, split-level

Of sticks, reliable heat.
Let stand, their sticks will freeze.
The cities will have to choose.
The future is nothing more
Than its own revenge on the past;
The horizon lets its smoke up, out of bounds.
The evident strength which spreads

Us out from place to place, place to no place
Through cracked winds of pollen and heavy winds of
Gasoline, cannot know its own
Mind. High baritones, the trucks
In squads rush & perpetuate
The barrier lanes designed for them & theirs.
You and I have no share in the world to come.

OUR HISTORY

after Jaime Gil de Biedma

What else can I say about my country,
this country where the worst of the evildoers
win popularity contests, and the poor
crowd into the army, and bad government
is like the air, a faith, a way of being,
the goal and meaning of our history?

In the rickety pile of tales called history
the most ridiculous now describes our country.
Here's how it ends: as if we were one human being,
we have announced, "I'm tired of evildoers;
I'm just going to let them buy the government.
That will exhaust them. That will make them poor."

The rest of the world knows how we treat our poor:
we give them a chance to get rich. If they blow it, they're history,
and it's off to jail with them. We don't blame the government—
that's part of what we love about our country;
we're all too busy fighting evildoers
to notice the stale crusts of bread at the core of our being.

It's an old problem: how do we go on being
so comfortable, and so troubled? Are we poor
losers? Am I one of the evildoers?
Often I imagine another history,
in which our stumbling, misbegotten country
learns to tell the truth about the government;

I try, at least, to imagine that every government
simply reflects the decisions of human beings,
that no magician's curse has befallen our country—

no one has cast a spell to keep the poor
locked up, nor raised the whole dead history
of empires stretched till they snap by evildoers.

I want to believe there are no evildoers,
only men and women in government
who hold and obey their beliefs about history,
for whom buying and selling, and being
bought and sold, are no reason to send the poor
home in coffins. . . . Then I look at the country.

I too would like to be rid of the evildoers,
but for now this country likes its government.
What will the poor nations say, when they write our history?

OVER LONG ISLAND

for Tara Emelye Needham

A swept rock garden. With an enormous rake
The lines of pebbles—roofs—have been made clear:
Their parallels leave rivulets, and bare
Calm soil along one edge, the Sound. Severe,
Like any rock garden in winter; so try to make

Its scale, its thumbprint creeks and springtail lakes
Bespeak
Not how smooth stones or snowflakes look alike
But what they thought they found when they came here:
Clean sidewalks. "Freedom from want. Freedom from fear."

THE WHISKERY TOWNS

If our
business with
the world
        fails,
we'll end

        up here:
expansively
dilapidated
        Weatherfield, Maine,
somewhere the train shoots through.

        Cattails. Sand
flats. New paint
against a dry rattan
        umbrella. The spent
moon's been out all day. . . .

        Parenthetical
little divers,
no snobs and not ambitious,
        careening
seagulls crowd the shore road's rails.

MIAMI BEACH

for Milton Heller & Esther Burt Heller

Perhaps the essence of being a Jew meant to live forever
in a state of expectation for that which would not come.

  —Irving Howe, *World of Our Fathers*

To end one's life and know it by degrees
Like the men and women in these pictures:
In their eighties in their Seventies
One shirtless blue jeans hooked over a paunch
With sun across his ribs their fine white hairs

The frequent naps the world too soon confined
To one square mile then a square half-mile
A woman framed by full-moon glasses holds
Her tiny opal earrings in her hands
The swept-back wings the mustard-colored steps

Front the last kosher hotel Here fame has saved
The nautical fins and sterns the turquoise curves
The edifices steaming in the wake
Of their expensive futures As for these
The shirtsleeve women men in iron chairs

The lucky the ocean-faced the escapees
Who squint and smile and grieve they face the sea
The Europe it has held with shaky hands
Who sat in the sun on balconies younger than they
And watched their language set all afternoon

OLD WOMEN AT THE BEACH

after Pablo Neruda

Before the heavy sea
          as if it were not a grave,
                    old women arrive, their slacks
rolled up around their thighs,
          their pale, respectful feet
                    like cracked and mended glass.
They settle down as if
          before an enormous ear
                    and never open their mouths;
they fix their eyes on clouds.
          The indiscriminate sea
                    rasps at them, and breaks;
they stay beyond its reach,
          and think of their narrow escape.
                    Asleep, the women feel
like passengers in some glass-bottomed boat;
          they glide over the poison
                    lionfish, the eel,
the dim, then sharp, abrupt
          and technicolor shoals.
                    Wherever they have lived,
they have their ocean now,
          their solitude full of noise.
                    They do not see the sea
but write on it with their canes.
          Each tide delivers their notes;
                    each moon comes up to read
the deliquescent scrawl above their names.

CHRISTINE WILLCOX: *FROG BABIES*

'alone I saw while whistling my third eye'
a sort of a summons

my own waterproof right hand

plunged into the surf to meet

inchoate and salt
the buoyant

O foam   erase and soothe
              comprise for us   some prokaryotic self

umbilical a new   life
                                        the old laid bare

split lost compelled dissolve a sort of a
                                song of a
                          siren sense
                    emerge and breathe
                    emergency
                    emerge and lose yourselves

the arc retreating waves leave
                              cold in sand

    webbed breathing   of visible touch
    round shoulders and a ribcage   open up
    some face   some separate   newness   some

                          recesses to

        this salted freezing air

NEAR NORTH

Broken-up sheet ice on the Chicago River:
its blue-green the shade of kryptonite,

dangerous leavings from an exploded planet.
The parallel hotels keep back the wind.

In the origin story of Superman,
his father straps the infant in his capsule,

frozen for a safe trip through deep space.
His rocket flees their home world as it splits—

tiny projectile, immense red sun,
tall narrow panels, a second-by-second arc.

Taut wires and pillars frame the swelling crowd:
its Saturday families, shoppers, conventioneers

and grown-up friends swing bulky shopping bags
along the edge of the city, against the lake.

A girl sprints over the bridge in a Superman sweater,
her candy necklace tight around her throat.

AT THE PROVIDENCE ZOO

Like the Beatles arriving from Britain,
the egret's descent on the pond
takes the reeds and visitors by storm:
it is a reconstructed marsh
environment, the next
best thing to living out your wild life.

Footbridges love the past.
And like the Roman questioner who learned
"the whole of the Torah while standing on one leg,"
flamingos are pleased to ignore us. It is not known
whether that Roman could learn to eat upside-down,
by dragging his tremendous head through streams.

Comical, stately, the newly watched tortoises
mate; one pushes the other over the grass,
their hemispheres clicking, on seven legs
in toto. Together they make
a Sydney Opera House,
a concatenation of anapests, almost a waltz.

Confined if not preserved,
schoolteachers, their charges, vigilant lemurs, wrens
and prestidigitating tamarins,
and dangerous badgers like dignitaries stare
at one another, hot
and concave in their inappropriate coats.

Having watched a boa
eat a rat alive,
the shortest child does as she was told—
looks up, holds the right hand
of the buddy system, and stands,
as she explains it, "still as a piece of pie."

"WHAT ELSE SHOULD WE SEE IN SAN FRANCISCO?"

Back and forth of prerecorded accordion,
back and forth with the inland-tending bay.
Sine and cosine. Red graph of the bridge.

❋

Eighteenth and Valencia, *borealis:*
a storefront of white fridges, none plugged in.
Quick balconies. White sky in the rain.

The absolute pale light of California
turns desperate and silver overcast.
Carved into the sidewalk: ODE TO JOY.

A storefront full of singled-out blue glass:
we don't like the money, but what would you put in its place?

❋

The fool's-gold-colored triple family home;
its neighbor with the simulated owl,
her wooden feathers splayed astride her tail . . .

The stop where all the girls get off the train
and all the tousled, glossy boys get on.

AFTER CALLIMACHUS

Sleep, Conopion, sleep
   as you make your admirer sleep
on the colder stones beside your bolted door;
sleep, Conopion, sleep
   without regrets, without a second thought
of the hardened and shivering man you don't want anymore.
If you wake, and stand, and see
   your lover prone under your window, and without
much hope of you to keep the chill away,
you'll surely go back to sleep
   and leave your neighbors to ask
what pitilessness could leave him there till day.

IV

"Bless me! what have you here?" said Wakem, startled by a sudden transition from landscape to portrait. "I thought you'd left off figures. Who are these?"

"They are the same person," said Philip, with calm promptness, "at different ages."

—George Eliot, *The Mill on the Floss*

ABSTRAKTES BILD

after Gerhard Richter

Erase the world   and you will find the world

Under a clutter   of sunlight Divest
Yourself of things   the snake the crop of sun

Invasive   in flight in the left corner flying
Blind   You know that these are not

Three columns supporting a story   These are not
Three poles of a trellis   three stakes for a gardener's vines

These have no creator   and are not
The gray slats of a window   nor the trace

Of crystallography in our machines

So give the weekend back   its silence and static and speak
To nobody   Stay in Colors of basil and ash

These things are always yours   have always been

There was nothing outside   and then   you saw them close the doors

SIX KINDS OF NOODLES

You would have to have been reading John Ashbery
to have seen anything like this in a book,
and yet here it is in real life:
an almost already intelligible tangle
of verities, and an intimidating menu,
disfigured, almost, by all the things you can have

at once, though all are noodles. Have
you, too, been trying to keep up with John Ashbery?
Every time I check there's another new book,
another entry—entrée—on the menu
from which I seem to have ordered my whole life,
and been served somebody else's. Don't tangle

with waiters here is my advice; the rectangle
of mirrorlike soy sauce, the soba you have to have
and the udon you lack should suffice: the secret of life—
as you might have sought, or discovered, in Ashbery—
is what you get while you are waiting. Men, you
see, are mortal, and live to end up in a book,

though once you compiled and published such a book,
who would be left to read it? The latest angle
claims that it would be more like a menu,
an ashen, Borgesian checklist of all you could have
or have had to pay for, or suffer, or notice. Ashbery
could write that (I think it's in *Flow Chart*). And yet the life

we long for in all its disorder is not a life
of so many tastes, nor of fame; more like one good book,
and ginger with which to enjoy it. Jeffrey Skinner's poem entitled
    "John Ashbery"
and David Kellogg's "Being John Ashbery" both take the angle
that eminence is what matters. No. We have
had enough of fighting over the menu,

as if it were the main course; the omen you
seek, the bitter-lime tang of a happy life
to come, curls up amid the semolina or buckwheat you have
not chosen yet. Will it be prepared by the book?
Will it do for Kitchen Stadium? Its newfangle-
ness may be a virtue, Iron Chef Chen Kenichi, Auden and Ashbery

all suggest, though hard to find here without help from Ashbery:
it's a problem with which I have tangled all my life,
and I'm so hungry I could eat a book, though none are listed on this menu.

ROSANJIN

(b. Kamigano, 1883; d. Yokohama, 1959)

All arts are one.
So what to serve in cobalt-fired leaf,
crosshatched ellipse, or broad enameled square?
How should one slice pale turbot washed in frigid water—
thick on a grey day, fine when there is sun?

He often remembered aloud his days in bed—
aged seven, mortally ill,
curled up and heaving, scar-pale, and craving

mud snails.
So his mother quarreled with the doctors,
who reasoned that he'd die soon anyway;
thus persuaded, she brought

mud snails.
He recovered fully, if slowly.
To this day I am fond of mud snails.

At ten, he stood still, near shock
in the path before the market,
overcome by awe
at the glistering cylinders cut from wild boar.

Wanted: second cook
for Hoshigaoka, 1934.
Required: passion. Must have been judged "eccentric"
from your devotion to food.
Required: excellent health.
Must invent food for each season and every year.
Must yearn to remain
famous for your cooking in times to come.

I came to ceramics through my love of food.
Delicious food required plates
to match. And so I took up lacquerware . . .
Here is a charger I made, a square
with raveled, rolling edge.
The cracks here show its history of use.

Most potters are artisans merely, neither proud
nor worthy of much pride.
Yet a bowl for tea, once dropped and smashed,
would merit no price at all.

The golden-tint *bonheur*
of a perfect square contains
a circular space where a few bright meals might go.

The crispy, curvy edges of soft eel.

I can no longer take pleasure
in dishes I have not prepared.
It is possible to know too much.

❀

People who want to eat well
have only to choose what they like
and prepare it as they like.
Most, however, have no idea what they enjoy.
So few understand
how flavors interact,
or know the work at all . . .

Photographed in the last
year of his life, he leans
impulsively over a screen
on which he writes in black curves, with a brush
whose bright length points straight up.
Advancing through him, every stroke he makes
reverberates—
                    Quick taste
whose patience and impatience work as one.

AFTER MONICA'S PARTY

Thickening square of sun on a swept board floor.
The beautiful nails, pounded down in pairs: heads up.

The scene all nouns, about to swivel and shift
to something almost coming into focus,
and always then beginning to turn away.

Roe in em-dashes over the last left plate.
The maplike, remnant folds of slept-in linen.

Compass and clock: both stubborn needles point
from San Francisco up and all the way home.

The scoured dishes in their warming racks,
the pneumatic feathery bits in window-glass,
the bearded irises in welcome languor,
the language of tulips inviting the coming noon,

and you asleep among them,
curled up around one elbow, the sun at your back
in long-awaited reverie,
landing and drifting among your new belongings.

FRANZ KLINE: *WANAMAKER BLOCK*

The shadow of a bottle on the wall
climbs the wall.

A death of uncertain provenance, like a lie.
A calm half-skull looks out for its lost eye.

RICHARD DIEBENKORN: *OCEAN PARK, 24*

Lovely you are, a shoulder, or a shirt

worn by a quietly irretrievable flirt

beside an open window. Bars hang at one end,

from which a practiced gymnast might dangle, or land.

CLEO

Nights I feel safe in your house. When the bit of thin air
The television leaves us threatens to cross
My path, and the nimble grey mate with whom I share
A food supply and a pillar of rattan and dross
Chases me out of my corner, I announce
My presence on or near your sleeping head:
I am the self-propelled, soft eminence
You knew before that strange and easily led
Man came to share you with me. I have known the black cloud
Of which you have lately complained, being myself
A short black cloud, and though I can neither pounce
On evanescent dejection, nor bury a rough
Insistent memory, I do announce
Some hope in my fur-lined fur undercoat's silver
Lining. I can lie flat
Like a seal, or curl up like a bear; a sudden, severe
If never quite silent presence at cuttings of meat
Or openings of fish, I race to assure
Or prove to you that strength of appetite
Persists in the absence of comfort, that some pleasure
May be seized even by those of us who cannot
Leap very far off the ground, or do more than growl
At keys in the door or far-off car alarms.
Though I see nothing I need be afraid of, still
I hate to be picked up, will scowl and bellow
And tether myself with one claw to cushion or rail,
Yet pad in ballad-rhythms across your pillow
And try at length to start each day in your arms.

AT CAPE MAY

      The shorebirds envy you, and the winds wrap
their contradictory tides
      around your bathing form,

      your royal purple
one-piece, as some sun
      catches you between waves.

      Traces of sand on your thigh
all gone in each new wash,
      salt blur in the air, add up

      to a beach where all things begin
again, are lust pinned down
      and built again as property, convinced

      that it alone knew better names
for having what we want. The black-billed tern
      who perches on our lunch

      no longer exists
in our world; he tries the crust,
      the citrus slice, the jam,

      and decides against them all.
His bill clicks, slight and sharp, ceramic on tile.
      He is content to have tested, and found us ill-

      suited to him, and departs
across our rolled-up towel . . .
      Is loving you an exercise

in tact and the accessible, a way
to learn just when to look, and when to touch?
        Or do the rapid elements

        of this shore town made young, its gaudy
traces across the jetty, see
        you as I do—a center,

        a beauty, a still place,
a determined look back, no girl's
        silhouette, but a woman who knows and decides?

PAPER ANNIVERSARY

for Jessica Bennett

      Pale rain retraces Chelsea, and a pale
receding sky the color of new bread;
      sharp buds on the new rosebush—pinks,
enticing whites: the same
      new colors as the flowers fully spread.

FRIGHTENING GARDEN TOOLS (INVADE YOUR DREAM)

Domesticity scares me: the pressure to make a grid plan—
A good plan—and saving, and knowing for what and for whom
Each act takes place. And yet the alternatives nod
Like split convictions, poles to ski between,
The hunches of derelict fences that nobody plays,

As one might play a wooden xylophone,
"Xylo" meaning "wood"; hence "wooden," redundant
Though also a needed reminder, like all these
Iced phrases, sills of houses we could choose
Or choose to live among. The frozen curves

And lines across the first roof cover
Themselves, then melt slowly, slovenly, in a surplus
Of effortful cousins' shovelings. Henceforth
I will accept the major premises;
I promise to take up this space, and to enter each act

On time and crisply, though across the way
Foxgloves proliferate, vans cough, and one
Chipped sunglass lens shines purple through the snow.
—There are risks involved, you understand.
—I didn't know you spoke French. —I don't, though I am.

JULY NIGHT

The child fears
    being caught, the adult

ineradicable disgrace.
    Our tangled-up and fertile garden fails

with raspberries, far more than we can pick
    before they rot or ripen for neighborhood dogs;

our hostas await their summer within
    a summer: capsule medicines,

differentiated once they bloom.
    Description hopes

for a place beyond itself;
    the sawteeth on our plum tree leaves are not

leaves but ideas,
    not only ideas, but a slap

in the face at the end of the day.
    Each sidewalk expands to a map

of the country, to a waste
    of handrolled cigarettes, things underfoot

or tangled among lost berries and much-provoked thorns.
    Acorns scatter like dice

in the driveways of next week;
    heroic ants carry twice their weight on sticks . . .

Is to be adult to be always
          disappointed, or to feign

satisfaction with what is? And these are the stars,
          as faint,

lucid and
          distant from us as our onetime hopes.

FIREWORKS

They have no theory. They just move
Up into the hour & split apart
Or get it over with; their one desire,
To fracture into incompatible sparks
& be extinguished, is what makes them go.

In that they resemble us, of course, how we use
Our years of hot pursuit
& regret them in whispers immediately, if at all.
Blue peonies, silver riding whips, tall spoons,
Corkscrews & trails of weeds,

They depend like everything else
Expensive or invisible on trained hands—
Italians, usually—whose flatbed Dodge
Will celebrate with stopwatches & beer
The successful completion of their appointed rounds.

The citizens watch, on lawns, through Labor Day,
Bay windows & emphysema, in rival schools
Or stand on benches as the city throws
What it can't forget up in thin air,
Kept safe by troughs of water, out

Of bounds. The recent past
Is opulent. The day
Wants only to last—chrysanthemums, speckled
Finales—yet eagerly turns
To ash and old news, over fields like a warning, a void.

AGAINST FERTILITY

This summer or Indian summer, with its tall
    or palely loitering, blurred
greens over drive-through banks,

    like any summer, is anxious: it is a test,
      from which the careful boys
hold back, preferring the bookish ice

    of earlier or
      lesser, later
days. Untoward squirrels

    in mazy stripes chase one another around
      our grocery store; asphalt in heaps,
and outdoor steam, and piled-up, yellowing

    melons in their way, set no
      distractions from their
trail of un-

    reserve . . . Because there are
      no new things under the sun, because we can't
make anything else of these, only more

    of the same, this summer turns
      uneasy. In whose name
was all this settled on us? Can't we stop

    and take
      good care of what we have? The riotous
French basil Jessie planted still explores

its own sharp outer reaches; in
        midair, our landlord's spider-flowers'
lunar-lander platforms lend their bees

    sweet targets for their last
        warm days. That none of them
may come to any harm,

    let school begin today; let everyone pass
        without increase. Let things stay as they are.

PHILADELPHIA

after Jorge Guillen

After the schemes, the scales
Of January and shade,
Elections and disgrace,
Dead leaves and getting by;

After the all-night drive
And signals in tunnels, lost
Behind the scrap of moon
And clouds like skin on a scar;

After the overpass
Of snow, the ragged cuts,
The poorly used concrete,
Huge fields and facelessness,

Here is the move you want,
The spring you awaited. Wrens!
Blackbirds and pigeons! Now
Auricular, as soft

As stern, and welcoming,
These cinnamon brownstones give
New evidence, opening
Inside the absolute

New season they promise. Stand:
Behold the adventurous crowds,
The wind, and libraries, and lanes
Where nothing remains of fatigue.

The soul, though loyal still
To the muscular body, makes
Its plenitude: the snow
Astonished in the hand.

AFTER CALLIMACHUS

By using no spice but salt,
Eudemus, once in debt—
hence mortal peril—changed
his ways, and saved his skin
from creditors' long knives.
Now kept afloat by thrift
as sailors by a raft,
he therefore consecrates
this salt-cellar to what
gods—humble and without
high monuments—permit
his business to go on.

NOTES

8 "Self-Portrait As Kitty Pryde": for the events the final stanza recalls, see *Uncanny X-Men,* nos. 141–42.

13 "For Lindsay Whalen" and "Help with Your Plant Questions": guard Lindsay Whalen and center Janel McCarville led the University of Minnesota Golden Gophers to the NCAA Division I women's basketball Final Four in 2004. Both players have since entered the WNBA, Whalen with the Connecticut Sun, McCarville with the Charlotte Sting.

16 "Scenes from Next Week's *Buffy the Vampire Slayer*" refers to events of the TV show's second season, in particular to the episodes "Phases," "Go Fish," and "Becoming (Parts One and Two)." My thanks to Rebecca Tushnet.

17 "Brief History of North American Youth": italicized lines in the second segment come from Joan Jacob Brumberg, *The Body Project* (New York: Vintage, 1998). The third uses late nineteenth-century diaries discussed and quoted in Jane Hunter, *How Young Ladies Became Girls* (New Haven: Yale University Press, 2002), adapting sentences by Alice Blackwell, Mary Boit, Marian Nichols, and Mary Thomas. The fourth segment quotes Kate Patton, and the last refers to the Washington, D.C., rock band Rites of Spring. Other parts of the poem owe their existence, indirectly, to Eric Meyer and to Rebecca Krupp.

25 "A Long Walk on a Weekday Afternoon" uses and endorses Girlprops.com (www.girlprops.com), now with two locations in lower Manhattan.

33 "The New Rock Jen" is Jen Matson. Grasshoppers and metropolitans are mixed drinks, the latter arguably invented at Marianne's, on Bowery; they owe to John Colburn their presence in this poem. For the songs the poem mentions, see the Chills, *Submarine Bells* and Interpol, *Turn On the Bright Lights.*

34 "'At the Bowery Ballroom'": for the song the poem describes, see Bis, *Social Dancing*. The poem owes much to Jane Yeh.

43 "Sixes and Sevens": the 2000 presidential election.

44 "Thanksgiving 2002": Senator Paul Wellstone (D-Minnesota) died in an airplane crash on October 25, 2002, twelve days before the election in which he might have won a third term. Minnesota voters then chose Republican Norm Coleman over the Democratic-Farmer-Labor Party's substitute candidate, Vice President Walter Mondale. For more on Wellstone and his legacy, see www.wellstone.org. Five italicized lines in the poem's third segment quote W. B. Yeats's poem "To a Friend Whose Work Has Come to Nothing."

57 "At the Providence Zoo": a curious Roman supposedly promised the Rabbi Hillel that he (the Roman) would convert to Judaism if Hillel could teach him the whole of the Torah while standing on one leg; Hillel supposedly replied, "Do not unto others as you would not have them do unto you." The poem also owes much to remarks by Amber Santacroce, Courtney Guntner, and Alexis Jarvis.

63 *"Abstraktes Bild"* ("abstract picture"): title for a series of paintings by Gerhard Richter; the poem also takes inspiration from Monica Youn.

66 "Rosanjin": see Sidney Cardozo and Masaaki Hirano, *The Art of Rosanjin* (Tokyo and New York: Kodansha, 1987), trans. Juliet Winters Carpenter. Italics derive (sometimes verbatim) from Rosanjin's own writings, excerpted and translated there.

Stephen Burt is the author of a previous collection of poems, *Popular Music,* which won the 1999 Colorado Prize. He is also the author of *Randall Jarrell and His Age,* which won the Warren-Brooks Award for Literary Criticism in 2002, and the co-editor of *Randall Jarrell on W. H. Auden.* His essays and reviews have appeared in the *Believer,* the *London Review of Books,* the *Nation,* the *New York Times Book Review, Poetry Review* (UK), *Slate, Thumbscrew,* and the *Times Literary Supplement,* among other newspapers and journals. He grew up in Washington, D.C., and now teaches at Macalester College in Saint Paul, Minnesota.

The text of the poems in *Parallel Play* have been set in Méridien, a typeface designed in 1954 by Adrian Frutiger. The poem titles are set in Gotham, a typeface designed by Tobias Frere-Jones in 2000. Book design by Wendy Holdman. Composition by Stanton Publication Services, Inc. Manufactured by Bang Printing on acid-free paper.